Read
a Zillion Books

by

Jerry Pallotta

Richard C. Owen Publishers, Inc.
Katonah, New York

Meet The Author

Text copyright © 2004 by Jerry Pallotta

Richard C. Owen Publishers, Inc.
PO Box 585
Katonah, NY 10536

Library of Congress Cataloging-in-Publication Data

Pallotta, Jerry.
      Read a zillion books / by Jerry Pallotta.
             p. cm. - (Meet the author)
      Summary: Jerry Pallotta, author of many alphabet books and other nonfiction works for children, recounts his life and describes how his daily activities and creative process are interwoven.
      ISBN 1-57274-597-5
      1. Pallotta, Jerry-Juvenile literature. 2. Authors, American-20th century-Biography-Juvenile literature. 3. Children's literature-Authorship-Juvenile literature. 4. Technical writing-Juvenile literature. [1. Pallotta, Jerry. 2. Authors, American.] I. Title. II. Meet the author (Katonah, N.Y.)

PS3566.A+Z475 2004
813'.54—dc21
[B]

                                                    2002074267

Editorial, Art, and Production Director *Janice Boland*
Production Assistant *Janet Lipareli*

Cover layout and page sequence by designer *Bonnie Gee*

Composition by Tandem Graphic Art Service, Mt. Kisco, NY 10549

Printed in the United States of America

9   8   7   6   5   4   3   2

Special thanks to my inspiration,
Neil, Jill, Sheila, and Eric

When I was a little boy, I loved telling stories
but I never thought about writing books.
No one in my family was a writer.

Massachusetts

★ Boston

• Scituate

In elementary school our class never kept journals,
I never wrote a book, or even imagined that I would,
or could, write one.

Here is a picture that I drew when I was ten years old.
My teachers told me I was a good artist.

But I would never become an illustrator.

In high school I never wrote for the school newspaper. I was too shy, I was afraid of what the other kids would think.

In college at Georgetown University I still never imagined writing books and I never wrote for the college newspaper. But I did love to read.

I married my college sweetheart, Linda.
After a few years we had four children.
Every day my wife would say to me,
"Please read to the kids!"

The first books that I read to my children were alphabet books and counting books.

One, two, three,
    four, five, six,
        seven, eight, nine,
            ten.

A was always for Apple,
B was always for Ball,
C was always for Cat,
and Z was always for Zebra.

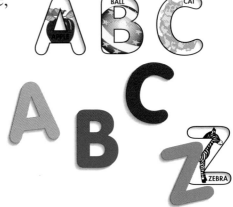

One day I made up different words.

"A is for Applesauce," I said.

"No!" said my daughter.

"A is for Apple tree," I said.

"No!" said my son.

"A is for Apple pie," I said.

"No!" said my other son.

"Honk!" said my youngest daughter.

Reading to my kids gave me the idea
to write my own alphabet book.
I wrote about my favorite subject—
the ocean!

I knew I could write the book. After all, I grew up at the beach. The Atlantic Ocean was my backyard.

As a kid I harvested seaweed, and I went clamming and lobstering just like my kids do today.

I went out on a dragger—a fishing boat that drags nets.

I even had my own dory—a small flat-bottomed ocean work boat. I did everything except sleep in it. Oops, I did sleep in it one night.

Here is the first draft of my first book,
The OCEAN Alphabet Book.
I tried to find sea creatures from A through Z
in the bay where I grew up. Let's see . . .
B could be for Bluefish. L could be for Lobster.
H for Hake, Herring, Halibut, Hammerhead shark,
Humpback whale, Hermit crab or Horseshoe crab.
Uh! Oh!

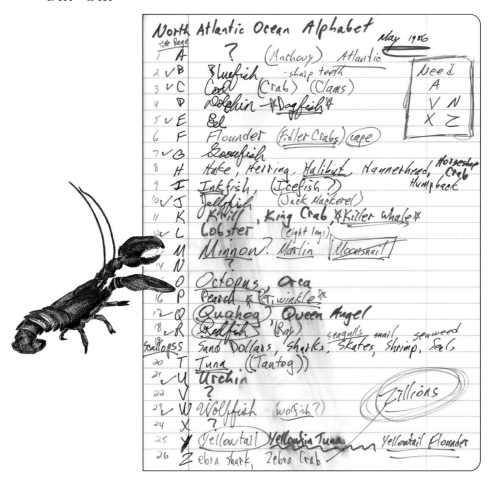

Here is what the *OCEAN ALPHABET BOOK* looked like when it first came out.

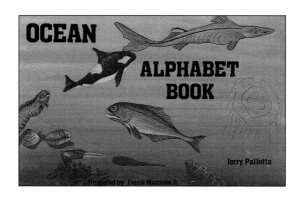

I came up with the idea, researched it, wrote it, designed it, edited it, and hired the illustrator. Then I published it myself.

At first, it was available at aquariums and museums around the country. It sold very well and that gave me the confidence to write more.

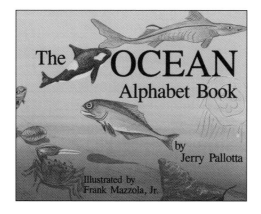

Now it looks like this.

I went on to write twenty alphabet books.
Millions of copies have been sold. What fun!

Sometimes it all seems like a dream
and I just shake my head.

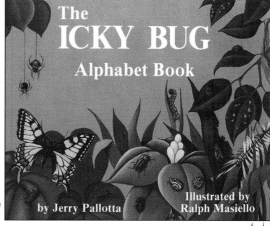

I was attracted to the alphabet
because you could read an alphabet book
with or without the text.
You could just read,
"A is for Ant,
B is for Bee,
C is for Cricket,"
or you could read
the whole text.

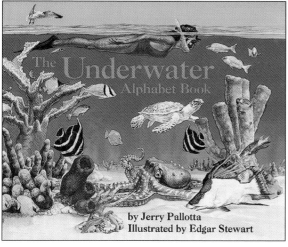

I also liked the
fact that there is
a beginning, A,
and an end, Z.

15

An alphabet book gives you a chance to tell
twenty-six short stories.
The alphabet is great for teaching information.

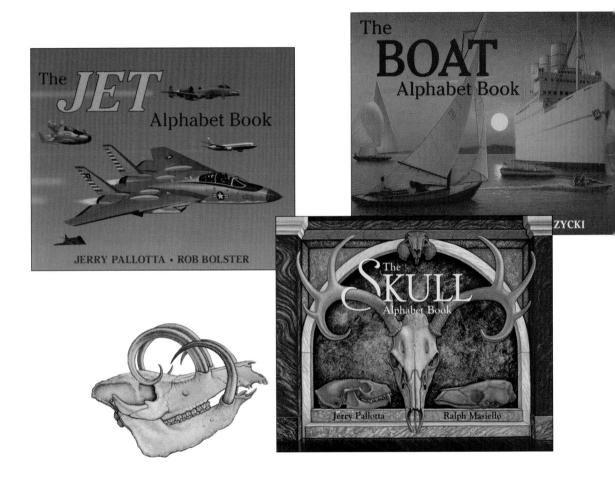

I think of my alphabet books as mini-encyclopedias.

I think about writing books all the time.
I want to create interesting, fact-filled, fun-to-read,
beautifully illustrated books for children.

Here are some of the other types of books I write.

If you asked me what my typical day is like, I guess
that I would have to say that I have three kinds of days—
days I spend with my family, days I spend writing,
researching and developing books,
and days I spend visiting schools,
speaking at conferences,
and signing books.

I love to research. And I read as much as I can.
When I get an idea, I write it down,
usually with a pen or a pencil on paper.
I write on everything and anything
and I don't work in a special place.

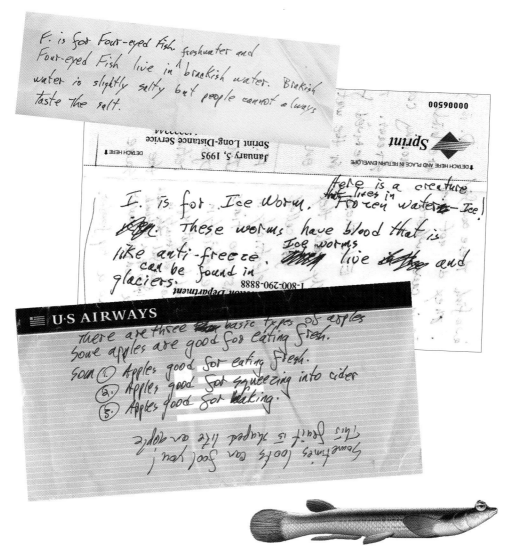

F. is for Four-eyed Fish. freshwater and
Four-eyed Fish live in brackish water. Brackish
water is slightly salty but people cannot always
taste the salt.

Sprint Long-Distance Service
January 5, 1995
DETACH HERE ↑   ↑ DETACH HERE AND PLACE IN RETURN ENVELOPE
Sprint
000065000
0005900

Here is a creature
I. is for Ice Worm. that lives in frozen water—Ice!
These worms have blood that is
like anti-freeze. Ice worms live and
can be found in
glaciers.
1-800-290-8888

U·S AIRWAYS
There are three basic types of apples.
Some apples are good for eating fresh.
Some 1. Apples good for eating fresh.
2. Apples good for squeezing into cider
3. Apples good for baking.

Sometimes fruit is shaped like an apple
Sometimes fruits can fool you!

After I write my story by hand, I type it. I edit it
and I type it again. Then, I rewrite it and rewrite it.

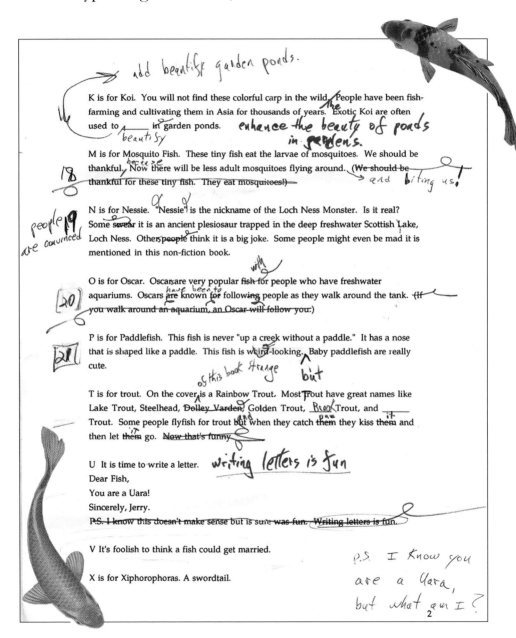

add beautify garden ponds.

K is for Koi. You will not find these colorful carp in the wild. People have been fish-
farming and cultivating them in Asia for thousands of years. Exotic Koi are often
used to _____ in garden ponds. *enhance the beauty of ponds in gardens.*
beautify

18
M is for Mosquito Fish. These tiny fish eat the larvae of mosquitoes. We should be
thankful. *because* Now there will be less adult mosquitoes flying around. (We should be
thankful for these tiny fish. They eat mosquitoes!) *and biting us!*

people 19
are convinced
N is for Nessie. "Nessie" is the nickname of the Loch Ness Monster. Is it real?
Some swear it is an ancient plesiosaur trapped in the deep freshwater Scottish Lake,
Loch Ness. Other people think it is a big joke. Some people might even be mad it is
mentioned in this non-fiction book.

20
O is for Oscar. Oscars are very popular fish *with* for people who have freshwater
aquariums. Oscars *have been to* are known for following people as they walk around the tank. (If
you walk around an aquarium, an Oscar will follow you.)

21
P is for Paddlefish. This fish is never "up a creek without a paddle." It has a nose
that is shaped like a paddle. This fish is weird-looking. Baby paddlefish are really
cute.
of this book strange *but*

T is for trout. On the cover is a Rainbow Trout. Most Trout have great names like
Lake Trout, Steelhead, Dolley Varden, Golden Trout, Brook Trout, and _____
Trout. Some people flyfish for trout but when they catch them they kiss them *it* and
then let them go. Now that's funny *one*

U It is time to write a letter. *writing letters is fun*
Dear Fish,
You are a Uara!
Sincerely, Jerry.
P.S. I know this doesn't make sense but is sure was fun. Writing letters is fun.

V It's foolish to think a fish could get married.

X is for Xiphorophoras. A swordtail.

p.s. I know you
are a Uara,
but what am I?

2

20

I read what I have written out loud.
Then, I read it out loud again. I show it to my wife
and to my children. I show it to friends and neighbors.
I try to get as many comments as I can.
Then, I rewrite it, again.

When I get stuck, I read. I read. I read some more.

I go to museums and aquariums,
talk to scientists, visit zoos,
and look on the internet.

Many authors never meet their illustrators.
But I like the team-approach and talk to my illustrators
all the time. We meet with each other as often as
possible. It is a wonderful give-and-take experience.

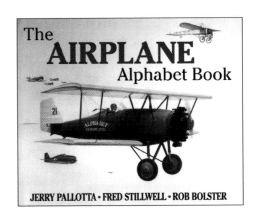

Here I am with Rob Bolster
who is showing me
some original artwork from
The AIRPLANE Alphabet Book.

I like working with my illustrators. Often, I act as the art director for my books, scribbling sketches and discussing how I want a page to look.

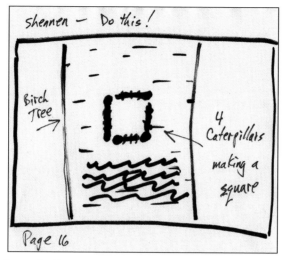

Here is a sketch I gave to illustrator Shennen Bersani.

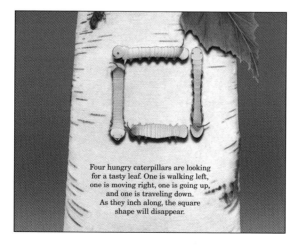

Four hungry caterpillars are looking for a tasty leaf. One is walking left, one is moving right, one is going up, and one is traveling down. As they inch along, the square shape will disappear.

Here is the finished page in *ICKY BUG SHAPES*.

That's me in the back of our family dory.
My nephew was rowing and I was designing a page
in my mind for *DORY STORY*.
David Biedrzycki, the illustrator for the book,
was up on a jetty overlooking the ocean.
He took the above photograph for reference.

Here is how it was illustrated in the book.

Ralph Masiello has illustrated seven books for me.
Ralph paints the old-fashioned way with oils on canvas—
except when he's drawing on my head!
He is really fun to work with.

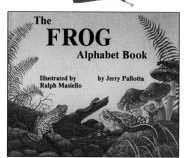

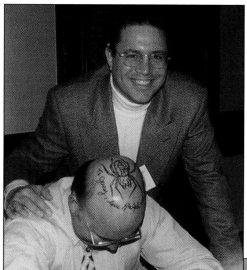

The
FROG
Alphabet Book

Illustrated by
Ralph Masiello

by Jerry Pallotta

When he was illustrating *The SKULL Alphabet Book*,
I got real animal skulls for reference.
Did you know that there is a skull store?

I always wanted to write a book about fractions.
When I heard that teachers use HERSHEY'S®
milk chocolate bars to teach fractions,
I asked permission to use the candies in my books.

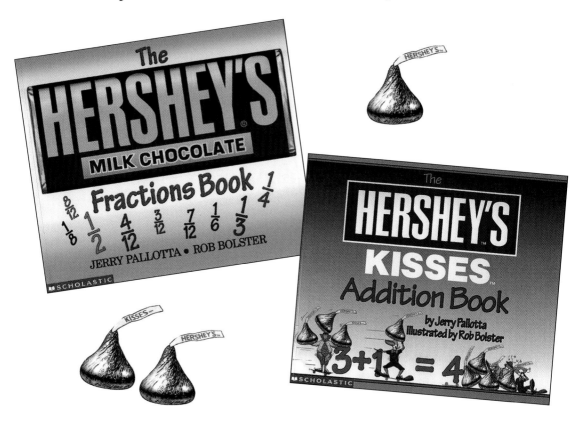

I've written about many other math concepts—
addition, subtraction, multiplication, division,
odd and even numbers, percentages, shapes,
and weights and measures.

Milk Chocolate + Math = Fun!

I am really proud of these books. They are multi-layered.

Kids can read them. They can do math. They can have fun and learn other things from them.

The multiplication book takes place in the art room.
The percentage book has aliens visiting from outer space.
The count-by-fives book uses construction equipment.
The division book has a sports theme.

A big part of my life is visiting schools.
Sometimes I speak to just one class,
but once I spoke to three thousand kids in a day.

I fly to cities all over the country
and have met with children in all fifty states.

When I'm not working on my books or visiting schools,
I spend my time with my family.
We do everything together.

It's true that when I was a little boy
I didn't think about writing books.
Now I realize that by telling stories all the time
I was writing books in my mind.

I still love to tell stories. I love to read and I love to learn.

Now that I am grown up I have the perfect job,
a job that I love.
I write books for children!
And I tell everyone I meet,
"READ A ZILLION BOOKS!"